POEMS ABOUT PERSEVERANCE

HALEY MARSHALL

Cover photo by Haley Marshall

ISBN: 979-8-9905462-8-8

Table of Contents

Table of Contents

Part One

Magic in the mundane

I will remember
Days like today –
I will love them now

I don't want to wait years
For nostalgia to appear –
I won't have to wait years
To cherish this moment.
Today I will acknowledge
The miracle of today.

I believe in magic in the mundane
Excitement in the everyday
Extraordinary in the ordinary

Ethereal success

Today I achieved
No tangible accomplishments
Only ethereal success

I found happiness
And built new things
Not tactile things
I built hope and faith
And patience

Hope and I

Have hope!
(They tell me)

Of course I'll have hope

I will seek hope
Run towards it
Chase after it
Hope and I
Will not meet by accident

Listing my worries

I wrote my worries on a list
(My mind began to run)
I dwelled on worries all at once
Instead of one by one.
It was no civil game of stress
No worry took its turn
When one worry walked my way
They all were a concern.

I wrote a list of joyful things
(It put my mind at ease)
And when I read the list out loud
My stress began to cease
There was no limit to my peace
My stress soon disappeared
And when my worries said hello
I knew they shouldn't be feared.

Narrating my dreams

I'm too tired
Of only outlining
These faraway,
Far-fetched dreams

Someday I'll write down
My faraway dreams
With detail so vivid
The dreams will feel real

If I narrate my dreams
With nuance,
Can my daring dreams
Turn into truth?

If I nourish my dreams
With effort and hope,
I think that my dreams
Can be lived and be loved

Built after failure

All of these things
I thought I could change them
I tried to improve them
I tried to succeed

I thought I'd gain wisdom
Once I had improved them
But I gained more wisdom
When failure met me

I gained new perspective
When hope helped me foster
A resolute spirit
Built from patience
(Not luck)

I built upon failure
I built after failure
And I'm thankful for how
My failure helped me

Joy must be shared, too

I lived in a happy neighborhood
A few blocks from sadness
Sometimes I walked
Toward unknown streets
And strolled by the sadness

I thought my happy neighborhood
Would keep all of its joy
I didn't know
That grief and gloom
Could visit my home, too

Next time I stroll
Away from home
And wander toward the sadness
I'll try to take
My joy with me
And share that joy with you

If sadness can be shared
Then joy must be shared, too

Well worth the price

You think I am early
In fact, I am late
You don't know what I've skipped
On each calendar-date
You don't know what I've canceled
Or what I've delayed
To be on time – here – now
There's a price I have paid

But to be here
Right now
It is well worth the price

Renew

Hope does not renew
On a schedule;
You can't look at a calendar
And precisely know
When hope will appear
But somehow
That idea seems hopeful
I don't have to wait for Monday
I don't have to wait for Friday
Hope could renew anytime
Tomorrow
Today
The next hour
The next moment
Right now

Wasting my worry

I don't want to waste
My worry on you.
I want to save worry
For opportune times,
When a dose of worry
Does a lot of good.

If something is scary
(A real and true threat)
I'll spend my saved worry
And look out for danger;
If something is scary,
I want to feel scared.

But if I spend my worry
On trivial matters
My worry may morph
And become a bad habit;
No, I'll save my worry
For opportune times.

A little piece of laughter

I have a feeling
Sometime in the future
This fickleness will fade

I won't borrow more sorrows
Or rent discontent
And I willfully won't
Possess more distress

No, I'll start to race after
A little piece of laughter

I won't be fast
But still, I'll grow
I'll find the self
I used to know

Close enough to reach

I am excited
About the existence
Of hope.
It is real
And right here
And close enough to reach.
It is something
I'll hold onto
And something
I can keep.

What tomorrow brings

So strange to think
How fast things can go
From a maybe
To a no

Yesterday we had a yes
And now we have a no

But today I will remind myself
What tomorrow brings:
Chance
And choice
And change

It's good to know
How fast things can change
From nothing and nowhere
To something and joy

Moving on

You shouldn't tell
A favorite friend
To move away from sadness.

She might be near
Her same old sadness
Because she's back to visit;
She may have moved already

Or,
Maybe your friend
Plans to move somewhat soon
(To move away from sadness)
But she needs time
Some extra time
To stay put
To stay here.
Moving on is a motion
And an emotion

If you're cold

If you're cold
Wear a jacket
Keep yourself warm!
I wonder if jackets ever get cold.
Do jackets tell their children
If you're cold
Find a human
Grab onto their arms
Warm yourself up!

Part Two

Meaning in the mundane

I wonder what a perfect day
Would look like –
Would it be one of leisure
Or excitement?

Would it be perfect
Because something great happened –
Because some change occurred?

Or maybe it's perfect
Because I finally found
Meaning in the mundane
Merit in the ordinary;
Because I finally recognize
The miracle of every day

Progress

Sometimes progress is slow
And failure is fast
Often failure will fade
And progress will last

I can work with harmony

I am trying to manage my stress
But my stress doesn't want a manager
It doesn't want a boss –
It wishes to do
Whatever it wants

I can embrace the idea
Of letting the stress go –
Of firing it;
I believe my stress
Should be employed
Somewhere else

I think it's time to hire harmony
I can work with harmony

Competition

She beat me
In a race
To the end.
She was not a rival
She is a friend
If we were rivals
I wouldn't care
But she's my friend
So I compare

I need to race
Against my own pace

Any other way

This piece of art is perfect
I don’t mean it’s without flaw
I just mean
I wouldn’t want it
Any other way.

I always know my art is finished
When I don’t want it to be
Any other kind of beautiful.

Here and There

It's often
Arduous
To make the first step;
To go from Here
To what will become
The next Here
(The new Here)

Every Here
Was once a There

Anticipation

Anticipation
Is sometimes
An unpleasant present.

I think I'd only like to see
That thing that truly frightens me
When it happens
(If it happens)

And if that very scary thing
That life may never even bring
Never, ever comes my way –
Then I'll be proud that I can say
I never truly tried to greet
A nightmare that I'll never meet

Embracing the unknown

I worried about the past
But I can't change the past
So I focused on the future

Then I worried about the future
But the future is unknown
And I found too many worries –
I couldn't figure out
What to worry about

I started to worry
About how much I worry,
So I found a new hobby

I like to call my hobby
"Embracing the unknown"

Small steps

Today
My small steps
Did not lead to large leaps

I found no success
(But I did not lose patience)

I made many mistakes
But I did not misplace
My calmness or my composure

I can find success
Another day
And when I find success
I'll be a gentler soul

Small talk

You say
You don’t like small talk
But I like small talk
Talking about little things
My day
Your day
Little things we like to do
Little things we’ve done this week

You learn a lot
About a person
By talking about small talk
You find out
Who
Wants to live in your world

Yesterday and today

I am not afraid of facing the day
Of greeting the day
Of saying hello to it
The day does not scare me

I just don't feel
Like spending time with the day;
Yesterday and I
Are still finishing our talk

I must remember
That I can be friends
With both yesterday and today

Now tomorrow is here
It calls itself today
And I won't act like it's a stranger
I'll greet it right away –
Because I already know
We are meant to be friends

To be calm

We learned to be calm
When peace was not present;
When a storm was the norm
We clung onto a psalm
(And hope was our balm)

You're free

I know you're worried
(About something next week)
But you're not under contract
To worry

You didn't promise anybody
That you'd be sure to worry
You didn't make any commitment
To fulfill your worry

In fact
You're free
To let that worry go

Ambitions

I awake
And yesterday's ambitions
Have changed into
The chores of today

But I know
I am certain
That today's ambitions
Will be the joys of tomorrow

Today's stressors
Would feel like stepping stones
If we only knew
The wonderful things that await.

Gather my thoughts

When I awake on dreary mornings
I must always decide
Which thoughts I'll take with me
As I go about my day –
Which ones I'll keep
And which ones I'll throw away.

I always try to carry
My very favorite thoughts
(As I go about my day)
And I always try to gather
Very happy thoughts
Thoughts I can keep
Thoughts I'll take with me
Tomorrow

Part Three

The pursuit

The pursuit of perfection
Is a terrible trail
I am tired of taking twists and turns
That lead to a few fabulous feats
And a long list of frustrations

I'm not trying to move to mediocrity
I just want to wander
To someplace wonderful

I don't want to treat
This season of life
As something I must shuffle through

If plans will not reveal themselves now
Then I will plan to revel in what's now

Almost delivered

Today I received
An unwelcome insult.
But if I could choose
I'd rather not use
The word "received"

The insult was delivered
Like a parcel in the mail
But I refused to sign
For the petty package.

So I suppose,
I never received
The unwelcome insult.
It was only
Almost delivered.

Photograph this feeling

I am gazing
At the gorgeous night sky
And I want to record
This marvelous memory

I don't need to capture
The words I say
As I look at the sky
I don't need to catalog
How the stars appear
As they look back at me
No –
I only want
To photograph
This feeling

Searching for something

I'm searching for stationery
I need to mail a letter
I want something pretty
And not too plain.
I want something with patterns
Something with motion
That shifts and soars across the page

I don't want to be stationary
I want to go somewhere
To a time and a place
Where there is change.
In an unchanging season
I'm searching for something –
I'm looking for patterns
That lead me toward change

A lovely place

this sadness
is something
that should only be visited;
we shouldn't move here

I'm going back home –
It's a lovely place
Where conflict doesn't conquer peace
And trials don't trample love

When Dread arrives

When Dread arrives
I acknowledge it;
I greet it at the door

I usually say:
Hello Dread!
I'm sorry you can't stay long
I'm sorry you're on your way out

(And then I ask it to leave)

Sometimes it doesn't go
Right away
But sooner or later
Dread announces its exit
Dread never stays very long

Something better

I am a magician
I can take a small concern
And turn it into a big worry

But I can also transform
A lousy afternoon
Into a lovely evening
When I take a few simple joys
(That the day has granted me)
And turn those simple joys
Into a spirit of contentment

Yes, I am a magician;
I can take a little disappointment
And push myself
To make a change
To change something big
To make something better

When Dread goes away

I have a tiny sense of dread
That I carry in my pocket.
I'll keep it for a while
Because what I fear is far away.

Someday I will face my fear
This little overwhelming fear
And once I've met it –
Once I've passed it by –
The fear will be gone,
And I'll wonder
Why I carried
That dread in my pocket
For so very long

Itinerary

I was unduly upset
When I forgot to follow
My present plans

Yesterday
I planned joy and peace
I did not schedule conflict

But then
I noticed
I had only scheduled morning plans
And the morning had already past.
I had not yet written
An itinerary for the afternoon

There was plenty of time to schedule joy
There was plenty of time to practice
peace

Defined

Today I was sad
And I called out my sadness
Called after it
Named it
Told myself what it was

Today I had anger
And I called out my anger
Ran after it
Named it
Told it to leave

Today I found joy
I called after that joy
Ran after it
Named it
Called it a blessing

Don't steal my joy

Don't steal my joy
Please share my joy
Please share this love and laughter

Don't steal my hope
I'll give you hope
I hope you'll hope with me

You can copy my contentment
You can plagiarize my peace

But please don't steal
My precious joy –
I'll share my joy with you

Meant for me

I try to plan
All that I can,
But sometimes life
Makes plans for me

Who knew
That these roads
I did not want to see
(The ones that I rode
When the detour took me)

Would in the end
Actually be
The very roads
That were meant for me

Start now

Start now.
I wonder what would happen
If you simply started now.

Let's go ahead and look for
The adventures you might find
The places you can explore
The magic that will unfold
If you start now

Sure, you could have started before
But aren't you excited
About sharing adventures
And exploring new places
Right now?
There's nothing wrong with Now

Today is Here

Today
Is
A new day
A different day
A better day
A day with new perspective
A day with new chances

www.ingramcontent.com/pod-product-compliance
Lightning Source LLC
LaVergne TN
LVHW090537110826
845146LV00003B/1154

* 9 7 9 8 9 9 0 5 4 6 2 9 5 *